Love thro

CW00496048

Achelya

◎ _achelya_

Third printing edition 2023

PAPERBACK ISBN: 9798398808360

I am so thankful to my mom and dad for raising me and always supporting me. Also, I am so lucky to have the best sister and best friend in the world, Merve. Thanks to all my friends who have always been there for me in both the good and bad times.

Table of Contents

V

Introduction

LOVE IS FROM AN ANCIENT TIME
Love Is Above The World

When I look at Women's eyes, I can see the pain dwelling deep within; and in Men, I can sense them seeking more. I believe this has caused an unbalance in the energy between men and women.

Modern life pushes our souls away from us, and every day we feel less connected and less loved. Mental health problems have been increasing over the years, and with lock down, it has reached its highest peak.
I feel pain and cannot sleep sometimes because of this.

I believe that this book will allow spirituality to be more visible in the world and help to bring balance between the spiritual and material worlds. Only then can people free their minds, and humanity can go back and reconnect the bridge between the body, mind, and soul.

I believe that we should not shy away from illuminating what's in our souls; never! Your emotions are yours. Accept them, live them, and be in the present.

Feel everything that comes to you naturally, and start to read the signs.

Every good thing starts with love; love everything around you, alive or not. Love will change everything.

Part One

Sky

Because stars brought us together...

The Day

When he touched her,
She started to fall down
All she saw around was smoke;
Grey, black, and white,
Then she understood where she was
She was in his soul
After realising, she stopped falling down
And looked around
She was herself in a beautiful place
Sky was full of stars
Where she was looking at
All the ground, under her hands
There were small, shining, colourful stones...
She shouldn't forget any details.

Vacation for My Soul

Miss me, baby,
'Cause I'm missing you.
Wherever we'll be,
There will be rest for me
'Cause you're a vacation for my soul.
My spirit is at peace around you.
My light is beaming.
I know you see that.

In my dreams
You look at my eyes
And talk to me.

Talk to me more, baby.
I need that, my love.

Next and Next Lives

We found each other in this life.
I know that
We will meet again in the next and next ones,
Like we did in previous ones.
Your eyes are familiar to mine every time.

The Story of Wolf and Panther

My soul,
We met in a different dimension again.
You are the grey wolf,
I am the black panther.
We walked together a little bit.
We hid from others in the cave.
Our souls were together
Under your grey fur.
Time to go now.
The wolf should look for something new,
Should experience some cold to see his fire,
Should go to the mountaintop alone.
Then he knows where the panther is
In her dream world, having a rest,
Climbing the tree, swimming in the jungle river,
Waiting for him.
She knows he will come back.
She knows he misses her.
She knows he belongs to her.

Waiting for You

I am waiting for you
As excited as the winter
Before turning to the summer,
As peaceful as the tree
Just accepting the weather,
As curious as a pigeon
Searching around and around.

Mask

Every morning I decide
Who I'm gonna be that day.
Choose clothes.
Wear makeup
Or no makeup.

If I don't know
Who I am today,
How can I show myself?

If the mask is wrong,
Can I choose the other one
Easily?

Melodies Are Dancing

Raise the energy.
Let me put on my body.
Feel every cell,
Catch every part of my soul.

Life is music.
Don't you see the rhythm?
Love is a symphony
Going up and down
But always magical.
You can't resist.

Melodies are dancing in the air.
Don't you see?

*I don't need to be an acceptable person.
I only need to accept myself.*

The Dream World

When I fall into the dream world,
You think it's easy to come back into the real world.
When you fall in love,
You think it's easy to find balance again,
And who wants that?

Balance

How much happiness can you take?
You will take that much sadness.
So, do you want happiness or balance?

What Is Love?

I can't say
"I love you, babe."
Love is not enough.
What is love?

Souls Are under the Skin

Who put our souls into bodies?
Is it God?
That's why we are suffering.
Souls are imprisoned
Under the skin
Set my soul free again.
Our souls
I will shine
With stars.
I will go
So far away
I will get lost
Again.
I will find you there.
When I come back,
You will be here
Again.
When we die,
Will we find absolute freedom?

Are You My Dream Man?

Are you my dream man?
I found you in pain,
Broken man,
Waiting to be fixed by me,
Waiting for my healing.

Are you my dream man?
Your hair, long to make me touch it.
Those eyes, meaningful to make me whole.
The beard, ginger too make me watch The Shining.
Your shoulders, wide to hold me better.

Are you my dream man?
Who can respond to my soul?
Who reminds me of me?
Who can see my magical side?

Yes, you are my dream man,
All dust, but clean,
All dark, but full of sparkle,
All in deep but happiness around.

Go Back to the Deep Side

I have access to the dream world tonight,
My need to see your eyes,
My need to wake up next to you.

Don't leave me alone
In the deep.
You are my light,
Illuminate me.
You are my fire,
Warm me.

You made me go back to the deep side.
Don't leave me alone there.

Love Purple

That's God's play.
No one wins,
No one loses.
Just try to live the best you can
Everyday,
Every life.
Enjoy blue,
Enjoy red,
Love purple.

You left part of your soul here to sleep with me.

Lost

You may think that I'm lost,
But I see the way clearly
Like I haven't seen before.

All the Time

Your sound in my ears,
Like an angel's whisper
All the time.

Your touch on my skin,
Like a phoenix plume
All the time.

Your eyes on my eyes,
Like a fire's smoke
All the time.

Creation of Love

Creation energy,
Pain and passion
— Never enough.
What you do,
No matter
How much more you put into it,
You want more and more.

Like our love, baby
We're creating that love.
We're drawing on endless papers.
We're writing poems on pages
From the sky to the roots of trees.
We're dancing in all dimensions.

Soul Underwater

You found my soul
Underwater.
You brought it back
To daylight.

You started to break chains
All around me.
You kissed me,
You opened my eyes.
Music plays in my mind
When you are around.
You changed me.

Wish to River

Have you ever made a wish to river?
The water becomes clouds
And falls over the ground.
Are you ready to feel the rain?
Have you ever seen the power of drops?
Are you ready to open your eyes?

Have you ever made a wish to trees?
The water touches leaves
And feeds the roots of trees.
Are you ready to feel divine energy?
Have you ever touched the soul of nature?
Are you ready to open your palms?

Get ready—
Nature is waiting for you.

Fly Tonight

The bird is free now.
She can fly now.
She can sing now.

Where the limit ends in your mind,
We're gonna fly there tonight.
You're gonna feel the wind of her wings—
Wind waves are gonna splash to your face.

Belongs

My body belongs to nature.
My soul belongs to him.

When you stop searching,
you will find your soulmate.

Panther Feel

Panther is walking.
Nobody is familiar.
No one is a stranger.
Everyone is in your order.

No one is valuable
to love or hate.

There is no limit, no before,
no after.
It's all yours;
choose what you want.

No one can hunt you.
You can chase all of them.
You are the most beautiful,
With all your darkness.

Trust Mother Nature

It's time to go back to nature.
Touch the leaves of trees,
Stop measuring the time,
Hear birds sing.
The wind is stronger but real.
See?
Time is slower now.

It doesn't matter who is alive tomorrow.
Our souls will be saved in time.
Trust Mother Nature.

With You

The world is so beautiful
While I watch you.
Making you happy
Makes me happy.
I wanna see that smile.

Shortcut

Did you see death?
Did you see what you regret?
What do you miss?
Who do you miss?
Who do you love?
Did you see the end?
Did you touch the edge?
Did you see your dreams there?
Falling?
Did you look for a shortcut?

Many Levels

Welcome to my world.
Do you like it?
What did you find in the deep?
Did you like it?

I've lived life
On too many levels,
And I'll continue.
No one can stop me.

I love life;
No one is an obstacle.

I wanna see.
When I try,
No one can change
How I think.

My Plant

I asked my plant
If I am alone.
She said no,
As long as I water her,
As long as I give my love to her,
As long as I kiss her every night.

Achelya

Tree Talking

I went to the park with all my anger.
I watched the leaves of trees,
felt the cold ground soak up my energy.
Then I touched the tree.
It revealed my heart full of your love.
I cannot desert you.

I saw your eyes whisper spells,
Your hug shows me heaven,
Your sex takes me to another dimension,
And I cannot abandon you.

I sent my energy to you,
I touched your body with my magic,
I kissed you,
I know you're missing me more now,
And you will come back.

Nothing can change everything.
But time.

Nature

Birds are singing,
Don't you hear it?
Mother Nature is putting a spell on the grass,
Don't you see it?

Under the Moonlight

My infinity,
My love,
I looked for you under the moonlight,
But I couldn't find you tonight.
I'm suffering.

Touch me in the moonlight again.
I don't mean just tomorrow,
I want you tonight,
Tomorrow night,
And every night.

Ability to Love

Everybody has beauty.
Every woman,
Every man
Has some ability to love but not to fall in love.
I'm ready to give
All my existence to you only,
And you are ready to take it all.

My Spring

How the spring comes to the world,
You come to my world.
My soul has flowers,
Clouds going,
Everywhere blossoming—
Pink, green, white, yellow, red, blue.
My smile is shining,
My body is warm,
I'm sunbathing in happiness;
I know you don't turn it into autumn.

Dark Night

I asked the night,
"Why are you so dark?
Why so deep?"
Night said,
"To show you your inner woman,
What you hide in the light."

Winds all around the world
Will help me.
At the same time, cold and hot weather
Is with me.
It will be raining,
And I will be accepting everything as a gift
of new life.

What you don't understand makes you sad.

Anywhere

I know now
I can't go anywhere.
Nights we spend together,
They always whisper
I can't go anywhere.
I touched you with magic;
You can't go anywhere.

Over Stars

That love is bigger than me
Because we met
Over stars.
I go mad
Sometimes.

We Were in Dreamland Again

We were in dreamland again,
Where you don't see with your eyes
And our souls catch happiness.
You drugged in me again
With your love.
You made the time move fast again.
Our love is bigger than time,
Stronger than time.
When you are not around me,
Time tortures me.
I feel physical pain.
I call your soul.
We spend time together in my dreams.

Visiting Heaven

Sex is intense.
Your touch goes to the deep.
Sleeping together is visiting heaven.
Waking up with you,
Coming to a new dimension—
How many levels
Can we live in?
No one knows the answer.
We will find another one every time.
Time will be different every time.

After Me

I am your happiness.
Do not deny it,
I see into your eyes.
They've changed
Since seeing me.

I'm your relaxation pill.
Do not deny it,
I feel in your arms.
You hold me better.

Timeless Love

Find me again when we turn to light.
I wanna explode with you in the heart of a star.
Again, we should dye the universe together.
We will meet again around the nebula
We will come to the world
And find trees.
We'll find bodies—
Bodies gonna find each other.
Timeless love.
Timeless and placeless.

Achelya

Water and Fire

Love is
Where you lose yourself,
Where you find yourself
Being one in two different persons,
Feeling freedom in a cage,
Losing happiness,
And finding better joy after
Seeing brightness in darkness,
Being water and fire at once.

I learnt to forgive everyone except myself. But I'll learn.

No One

I wanna be nothing.
I wanna dissolve in nature.
I wanna burn my body in the sun.
I wanna splash my soul to everywhere.
I wanna go from that world.
I wanna become a new woman daily,
A woman who sees a new world day to day.
Then I wanna die.
I can already feel my soul in the light.
I can already feel I'm in a new body,
A strange body.
It reminds me of the old ones,
That it's temporary.
It reminds me
I'm no one.

Light

I have a light in me
So powerful
It can't stay in.
It's all around me.
Wherever I go,
I'll light the space.

Conflict

Life brings you sadness
So you exist in happiness.
Life brings you clouds
To make you enjoy the sun.
You cannot love days
Without nights.

My Tree

"Do not judge me when you see me in the summer," Said my tree.
"I was here when it was winter,
Look at my curves
Up and down.
Life is not easy always.
I went underwater sometimes.
Look at my young branches.
They are the results of old skin.
Always move forward.
You will find your way always.
Do not stop dreaming."

Achelya

Play

I can play with everyone
But not in every way—
But with you,
In an intelligent way,
In a sexual way,
In a funny way,
In a spiritual way.
I love to play with you in every way,
And you love to feel the play in every way.

Speed of Light

When you reach the speed of light,
You will turn into energy.
So, this is your soul.
You can travel all around the universe.
When you stop travelling at the speed of light,
You will come back to your body.

Love through the Light

Stop pushing yourself.
Take a break from everything.
Find peace.
Feel your breath.
Feel you're alive.
Understand your body is a gift
In the timeless universe;
Enjoy your gift;
Stop counting your days.
Your soul is a light,
And light is infinite,
Able to travel everywhere
Just see everything as a light.
This is what you can do as a light,
Then you find a body
To live in
To see the universe with eyes,
To touch everything with the tip of your
fingers,
To listen to music,
To pray.

You will be a light again.

Love through Light

Stop suffering.
Enjoy your greatest gift—
It's your body.
But when you find somebody,
All the time will fly together.
Actually, not together.
If you always fly as one light
And then split into two different bodies,
You won't find peace till
You find each other.
And it is not going to be easy—
This is a unique experience
We have together, baby.
Proof of infinity.
No one understands,
Except for the ones who understand love
through the light.

Melodies

I just wanna dance
In my dream world.
Melodies are dancing on the air—
See from my eyes,
Touch them,
Be thankful for nature.
Life is pure heaven.

The person who doesn't cry alone
will not see the peak.

Without Regret

I wanna try everything.
Thinking is not for me,
No one can change how I see,
And I will die
Without regret.

Moonlight

I have a pain:
I come back home;
You're not here.
I'm on my own.
Let's start to live together
On that full moon.
Just say you want to—
You won't regret it.
I'm praying under the moonlight,
My sugar.
I'm falling down.
I didn't take you yet.
My veins want you.
I'm praying for you
Under the moonlight.

Drowning in Infinity

Nights without you,
Like not living at all.
Sleeping next to you,
Like drowning in infinity . . .
Spending years there
In one night,
When I wake up
My soul is so mature,
All answers found.
My body is renewed
With your love.

Lost

I don't know how long
As long as love exists.
My heart will be burning,
My mind lost.

Brightness

I can see the energy
In the darkness;
I can feel the brightness
In the light.

The Devil wants to see you tonight.
Get ready for all sins.

Achelya

Don't Forget

You are changing;
I can see that into your eyes.
Fucking small things,
But we like them.
Now promise me
You won't forget who you are,
That you won't forget our love.

When you have new personalities,
Make sure you're building on the old one.
Don't break yourself.
Don't let me go.

Artist

Because I love us
More than me,
More than you,

Be your artist in your own life.
Draw your way.

Listen

I already miss you.
It's like it wasn't you
Who I spent time with
All day.

I know your eyes are calling me
From deeper and deeper.
Listen!
Your soul misses me.
I wanna sleep next to you again tonight.

The Happiest Sunset

The happiest sunset
With you:
The sun is bleeding
Around in red, purple, and grey
And a little bit blue.
Red turns to black slowly,
Darkness comes slowly,
But I'm happy,
Peaceful in your arms.

Part Two

Earth

Hurting

My heart is hurting physically,
Getting heavier every day.
I cannot carry it anymore.
It's pulling me down;
My energy is soaked from my shoulders.

I can't live without you
'Cause you'll never be just a lover.
You're my soulmate,
Happiness.
You're the person
Who I can see in the dark
And in the light.
And I love you.
We can't break up.
Come back.

We're always scared to lose each other.
It damages us.
Come back.

Small Lights

Angels warned me
I didn't listen.
I choose to believe in small lights.

Pain

You are always in your way.
You didn't mind my screams.
You close your ears.
You look into your pain, always.
I've seen it.
I helped you, despite my pain.

I don't know who I am now.
I've been spent my time on you.
I've changed a lot.

I know your eyes are upset.
I know you better than you.
I don't know if I want you to be happy or upset;
They both hurt me.
I don't wanna know anything.
I don't wanna see spirits around.
I lost the reality totally.
I'm just living now.
I'll keep loving you in my dreams.
I'll keep missing our happy days.

Reality

You will find
What you're looking for in me
Because there are many
Love songs that lost their meanings,
Colours turned into reality.

I will never, never, never be enough.
You always seek more.
I set you free from yourself,
And then I had to go.

Find Reality

Lost my reality.
Trying to find back every day.
It's all right working
But wasting all my energy.
It's all right.
It's worth it.

Falling into the Darkness

I know there is a good soul
Under that skin.
I feel that.
Your eyes make love with mine
Every night.
I can't sleep without you
Anymore.
Don't let me fall.
Please,
'Cause I need you.
I'm waiting;
Don't let me fall into the darkness.

I just started to see the light.
The sky is blue;
Clouds are red again.
The night is coming slowly.
Don't let me live in the darkness.

Time is enough *for everything.*

Perception

Your life is your perception,
Don't confuse it with others'.
But life flows
Without anyone's perception.

Loyalty

If you understood all songs
With somebody . . .
I just wanted one body.
He didn't satisfy me.
I just needed loyalty
But couldn't see
I had to say goodbye
To my love
With my heart still in pain.
Yet I miss seeing red lights
In your soul;
I'm missing spending time
With your soul over the many hours
In a minute.

Wonder

I have a thousand emotions
At the same time:
Anger, hate, happiness—altogether.
But mostly wonder what you feel,
If you're broken,
If it's hard to talk to me.

Don't look into my eyes again;
I'm scared.
Intentions are in your eyes, still;
They didn't go anywhere, I can see.

I know you are my soulmate.
Your eyes told me again.
Even that's not enough
To be together.

My Soul Calls Yours

I'm tired
Because love fucked me up.
I'm scared that
if I can't find that happiness again.
I don't know
how I complete my soul again.
Since I saw your eyes,
I'm suffering without you and with you.
I know my soul calls yours.
I always know
When I am going to come across you.
While I try to suppress my emotions,
I see how deep they are.
They seem impossible to lose.
I guess I need to learn to live with them.
I wanna spend one more day with you.
Please ask me.

Fire

Fire will burn all the negative energy.
It will bring us to now.
You will release your mind.
Tell me
The truths you believe in
And the lies you tell yourself.
I will set you free.
I will return your present
While I touch you with my energy.
Just leave yourself to me.

The Attraction

I wondered
And still wondering the soul
Behind those eyes
They shine and take me
To the other dimension
I know when
I'm gonna see you
They come and whisper to me
Whispers I cannot ignore
That attraction made me mad
But I'm not gonna let it happen
Anymore.

Loneliness

I fixed your soul,
I prayed to save you,
But you hurt me all the time
In the relationship,
While we were breaking up,
After all of this, still.
Don't try to talk to me
Anymore.
Don't look into my eyes.
I need to be without you,
Utterly.
Now I need to be fixed.
I'm trying to protect my soul.
No one can help me
But loneliness.

Love angels whisper your name every day.

Lost Myself

I gave you my heart.
I gave you my soul.
I gave you all of me.
I lost myself.
Now I need to find my way back.

Bring Me Life Back

I feel like I am a woman again.
With my man,
I can't lose you.
Your touches bring life back to me.
They are deep and real,
Like how light strikes everything
And gives it life
With shades changing
Every second.

No Bravery

He has seen all women in me.
He has talked to them all,
Yet he is not brave enough
To handle them all.

Printed in Great Britain
by Amazon

32071935R00054